Introducing Cockatiels

If you are thinking of obtaining a pet parrot, and have been told that a cockatiel makes a lovely pet, then you have been told correctly. Indeed, in terms of monetary value you may be assured, no other parrot can compare with the chirpy, cheerful cockatiel. Here is a bird that is not only beautiful to look at and elegant in its movements, but is an ideal size, is extremely docile if obtained at a young age, and is quiet. Further, if you plan to have a mixed aviary collection, the cockatiel will live happily alongside even the smallest of finches—and there are not a lot of other parrots you could say that about.

Cockatiels are members of the large family of parrots, Psittacidae, and are native to Australia. They enjoy a very wide area of distribution within Australia, as do also the ever-popular budgerigar and the larger Galah cockatoo. They are largely nomadic, moving wherever there is water in the vast interior of the continent. They live in flocks which can range from a few dozen to a few thousand members—thus they are very social birds that enjoy company.

Their scientific name is *Nymphicus hollandicus*, and for many years they were thought to be a link between the cockatoos and the parakeets.

GW00370630

Your pet shop may have a Cockatiel Starter Kit which enables you to buy all the essentials at a pre-fixed bargain price. ◆

Regardless of the color of your cockatiel, they all make excellent pets which easily tame if you get them young. There are many color mutants and the bird shown here is a pied. See page 26 for information about pieds. ◆

Your local pet shop will have many general books on cockatiels. The book you are now reading is meant as a first book only and is far from *the last word* on cockatiels. ◀

However, it is now known that the only thing they have in common is a long tail. In most other features and characteristics they are cockatoos—aberrant though they may be. They do not in fact have any close relatives and are classified, like the budgerigar, in their own genus (a zoological rank or group).

The wild cockatiel (referred to as a normal) is essentially a gray bird with some white in the plumage. It has a lemon yellow face which carries an orange spot on each cheek—this is much brighter in the male than in the female. There is a little yellow crest of feathers on the crown, giving way to gray at their tips. The yellow of the male is more extensive than that of the female. The beak is gray-black and the feet are flesh to gray-colored. The underside of the tail is dark gray-black in the male and gray barred with yellow in the female.

Young birds resemble the female until they are about six months of age. They will then go through their first molt and the plumage of the male will show itself. Cockatiels are quite long lived and may attain 25 or more years—it is not unknown for one to still produce offspring as it nears two decades, though this cannot be regarded as normal. The size of a cockatiel will be in the region of 33cm (13in) and they weigh about 90g, so are very light.

Over the years a number of mutations have appeared and this means you can select from more

◆ This is a male pearl cockatiel. See page 27 for more information on pearls.

This mutant is called *silver*. It is uniformly colored a deep silver. ◗

than a dozen attractive colors, some quite spectacular, others less so. The best age to obtain a cockatiel is when it is very young but is feeding itself. This will be at about the age of ten weeks. At this time it is extremely receptive to being handled gently and will thus make a super tame bird.

If it is to be a house pet then most pet and bird stores will have a nice selection from which to choose—but insist on a young bird. If you wish to become an exhibitor or a breeder then you will

need to obtain stock from a reputable breeder who can guarantee you the genotype of the foundation stock you require. Obviously, the more attractive mutations will be more expensive than the normal cockatiel. The colors, however, have no bearing on the pet potential of a bird.

Cockatiels can learn to mimic a few sounds, and the male is generally better at this than the female. He also has a delightful warbling whistle not possessed by the female. This may be your first guide to the sex of a youngster, before it can be confirmed by the plumage color.

This is a cinnamon pearl female. See page 27 for further information about this color variety. ◄

◀ Special pacifiers are available for cockatiels.

(Above Left) An albino cockatiel in flight.

3

Feeding

It is no small coincidence that many of the world's most popular cage and aviary birds are Australian in origin. This is because in the arid terrain in which many of them live they must subsist on what is a very Spartan diet for much of the year. This fact enabled them to survive aviary conditions at the turn of this century when many were imported into Europe. At that time the nutrition of these then exotic birds was poorly understood. As a result, many birds from tropical countries failed to prosper—but the Australian species, such as budgies, cockatiels, and zebra finches, survived and even bred on what were often meager rations. This favored them greatly.

Unfortunately, because they survived, it was thought that such rations were adequate, even desirable. We now know this is not the case, because during Australia's rainy season their birds have access to a great variety of wild plants and fruits which the birds need in order to feed their young.

Seeds are the staple diet of cockatiels, but it is vital that they also receive a wide-ranging selection of wild plants, fruits and other items if they are to retain good plumage and grow to

The rare whiteface cockatiel. See page 28 for more information. ◂

Pet shops carry special foods for cockatiels. Do NOT feed just any kind of bird seed to your cockatiel, as they have special requirements. ▸

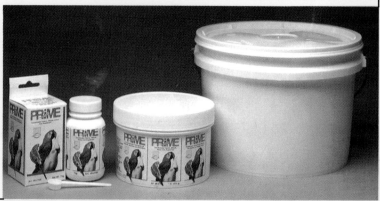

their maximum potential. Poorly fed birds will produce poor offspring. The cockatiel you purchase will have been bred in captivity, for there have been no export, of birds from Australia in over 30 years—this was banned, much to the dismay of breeders the world over. Your bird is therefore not wild caught and has been bred from generations of birds accustomed to receiving a well-balanced diet.

Feed your cockatiel a variety of cockatiel feed products. Your pet shop should have several varieties. ◄

Seeds

Cockatiels do not have especially powerful beaks, so they prefer small seeds. You can purchase budgerigar mixed seeds in packets if you have only one or two pets. If you plan to breed then it is more economical to buy individual seeds and make up your own mix. The bases of this should be panicum millet, white millet, and canary seed. To this other seeds, such as niger, sunflower, safflower, and the seeds of grasses, can be added in small quantities. Most cockatiels go nuts for millet sprays which can be given dry or after a soaking. However, use them as a treat, otherwise your pet may not want its other seed.

Ideally, it is best to feed seeds in separate dishes, as this will prove less wasteful. One of

Special treats and tidbits are also available to give your bird a treat. ◄

Do NOT allow your cockatiel to eat any fried foods—especially the junk foods that humans eat! ◄

Your pet shop has many kinds of cockatiel foods and treats. Discuss with your dealer the varieties and sizes. Obviously a large bag of cockatiel seed will cost less (per pound) than a much smaller container. ◄

Living World makes a complete line of cockatiel feeds which are supposed to correspond to the seasons in Australia. As the seasons change, so do the seeds and fruits available to the cockatiel in the wild. ◗

the problems with mixes is that it can happen that the bird has plenty of seed in its pot, but of a type it does not like (it having eaten those it likes). You think it is fine when it is actually desperately hungry. Likewise, with pots, these are often filled with the husks of eaten seeds. If the husks are not blown away daily you just might think the pot had a lot of food in it, when actually it had been empty for some time!

By observing which are your bird's favored seeds you can supply accordingly. If your pet is not very active, watch that it does not eat too many fat-rich seeds. They are not needed by such birds, so limit them. Never feed seed which is moldy or contains lots of dust—this is poor seed. Any rancid-looking seed is positively dangerous.

You will find that if some seed is soaked for 24 hours this will be appreciated by your pet, as will sprouted seed. After soaking you can wash the seeds and then place them in a warm, darkened cupboard on a tray of blotting paper for another 24-36 hours until small shoots appear. Wash again and feed. The birds relish these and they are good for youngsters and ailing birds that have gone off their food.

Grit

Birds do not have teeth so are unable to crush seed very well. To compensate they eat grit. This mixes with the seed in the stomach and churns the seed into a paste-like consistency. You must always be sure there is grit in the cage, either on

the floor or in a pot. You can obtain it from your petshop.

Greenfoods and Fruit

I will not list the potential greenfoods and fruit that your cockatiel will enjoy because birds differ in their liking of foods. You can work on the assumption that if a given vegetable, greenfood or fruit will not poison you then the same applies to your pet! Try it on a whole range of items and note which it seems to like. With wild plants the possibilities are extensive. Dandelion, chickweed, clover, shepherd's purse, yarrow and many others will be eagerly taken, roots and all. Obviously, avoid any you know to be poisonous—and wash plants in case they are carrying some sprayed chemical or have been fouled by dogs. Cockatiels will not eat large quantities of greenfoods and fruit but what they do eat is enjoyed and important to their well being.

Other Foods

Your cockatiel will enjoy bread and milk, maybe cookies (but try to avoid feeding sweet items), toast, brown bread, and many other items in your kitchen. If you take a common sense approach you will not go wrong. If the diet is varied you will have no need of multivitamin powders, which can actually be dangerous if used without a need for them.

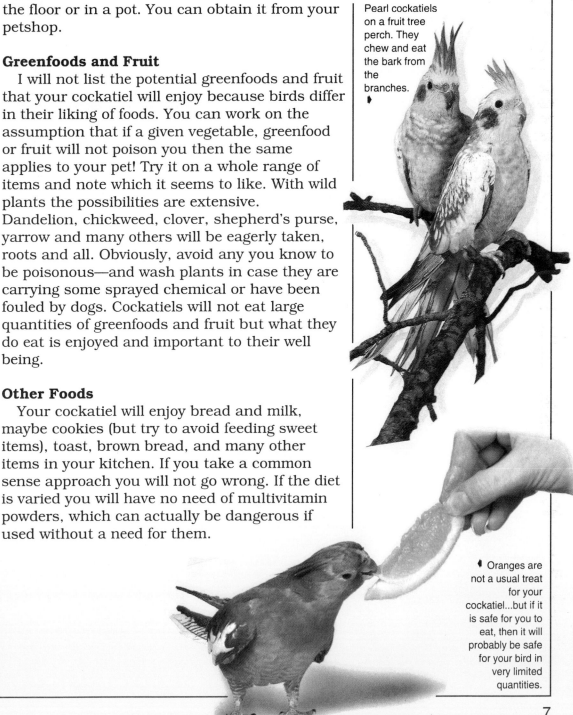

Pearl cockatiels on a fruit tree perch. They chew and eat the bark from the branches.

◆ Oranges are not a usual treat for your cockatiel...but if it is safe for you to eat, then it will probably be safe for your bird in very limited quantities.

A lovely mutant is the cockatiel called *bordered*. The bird above is a male. ◄

There are dozens of cages from which you can choose. But be sure the cage is designed for cockatiels with horizontal wiring and spacing tight enough so the bird can't get its head caught between the wires. ►

Accommodation

There are two ways in which you will wish to house your cockatiel. Either it is to be a house pet, in which case you will be wanting a cage, or you will be thinking in terms of establishing an aviary. This book is largely written with the pet owner in mind, but a few comments are given in respect to aviaries.

Cages

The most important aspect of any bird cage is that it should be as large as money will permit you to spend on it. Further, the ornamental cages offer no merit to the bird, so unless they are also spacious there is little to be gained in spending the extra cash on them. The very minimum size of a cage should allow the cockatiel to stand upright on its perch and have plenty of clear space between both its head and the cage top, and its tail and the cage floor. Anything less is far too small. It should also be able to fully extend its wings in order to exercise them.

These birds are not destructive or especially strong so you do not need the heavy metal cages made for the larger parrots,just a large cage. It must be stressed that budgerigar cages are totally inadequate for cockatiels, they are much to small. Cockatiels require enough room inside of the cage to flap thier wings without hitting the sides. A cockatiel's wing span is very large in comparison to the bird. It is usually double the bird's body length, including the tail. Being that cockatiels are approximately 13 in. long, their wing span averages 26 inches. A cage that is at least this size square will give the bird plenty of room to exercise within the cage comfortably. Square or rectangular cages offer more room for a bird than round or ornate, tall cages. The associate at your local pet store will be able to assist you in choosing the proper size cage. Remember, no cage is ever too big. The more space your pet has within the cage the better off he will be.

A good cage will have three perches in it, not two, and one of these will be higher than the others. Birds like to roost in the highest possible position. You can obtain suitable perches from your pet shop, or you can fashion them from apple or other fruit tree branches, which make ideal perches because their differing thickness provides good exercise for the bird's feet and also provides something for the bird to nibble on. As the bark becomes stripped it should be replaced.

The cage will need three feeding pots, one for seed, one for fruit and one for water. Actually, you could omit two of the pots and use automatic dispensers for seed and water, leaving one pot for fruit. Be sure the cage has a good-sized door fitted to it, and a secure fastener. Some cages are designed so that apart from opening the door you can open or drop an entire side to form a large landing platform.

The floor of the cage can be covered with a few sheets of paper, which can be removed one at a time as they become soiled. Some cages lift off their base to facilitate cleaning, which is a good idea. Always check the inside of a cage for any protruding pieces of metal. These can cause bad cuts to the wings or legs of your pet. Try to visit a number of stores before you make a choice—this way you will see more models.

Siting the Cage

The cage should be placed to take account of a number of factors. It should be free from drafts, so opposite doors is not a good place. It should receive sunlight, but not such that the bird cannot escape this if it so wishes. You can always create a shaded area using a suitable material. It should not be over a heating radiator which would result, possibly, in

A large cockatiel cage is best. This is an excellent cage. ←

Most cages come without baths. Add a cockatiel bath to your cage. Bathing is necessary for all birds. ←

A caged cockatiel is often bored. Add some chew rings to entertain your cockatiel. ←

Cockatiels, when allowed the freedom of the house, often attack the flowers. Many flowers are poisonous to cockatiels, so be careful. ◄

Dried cuttlefish bone is necessary as a calcium supplement and to help the cockatiel keep its beak worn down. ◀

Fresh water (at room temperature) is necessary for the bird to drink and in which to bathe if you don't have a bird bath on your cage. ▼

wide temperature fluctuations. This is a sure way to induce a chill.

It should not be too low. Your cockatiel will prefer to see you at about eye level or just below. If you tower over the cage as you pass it this will make your pet feel insecure. Placing the cage near a wall will give the bird a sense of security. Finally, cockatiels really do enjoy being part of the family, so place the cage where the bird can see what is going on in the room.

Remember that a cage can be a home or a prison to your pet, this being determined by how often it is let out. If you cannot let the bird fly free in your room very often then you should invest in a large indoor flight, or not have a cockatiel at all. It is always very distressing to see parrots cooped up in cages for most of their lives and makes you wonder why their owners ever obtained them in the first place. The whole beauty of these birds is to have them free and sitting on you where you will better appreciate their wonderful natures.

Aviaries

The minimum size of an aviary should be 3x1.8x1.8m (10x6x6ft). This would allow you to keep two to four breeding pairs of cockatiels, or some cockatiels, budgerigars and finches in a mixed collection. Serious breeders would not, of course, keep their pairs on a colony basis because they would want to control which birds paired with which. With this in mind you could reduce the width of the aviary somewhat. Likewise, the height of 1.8 meters is better for being raised somewhat in order that your view of the aviary is not spoiled by the

Aviaries must include natural twigs as perches so the bird can alight on different thickness of wood and thus exercise its toes and feet. ◀

◀ You can keep a cockatiel in a small cage for exhibitions and when it is ill, but an exhibition cage is not to be used for permanent housing.

roof cross member.

You will find it altogether more convenient to add a birdroom to the aviaries than simply to have shelters. The birdroom can be supplied with electricity and water, so you can attend to matters in comfort, as well as store all of the needed items and food. It can also contain internal flights. While you can purchase ready-made aviary units, most breeders find it better, and more economical, to build to their own design, maybe utilizing ready-made panels.

An aviary should include a safety porch, which is entered before the aviary proper is entered. This greatly reduces the risk of birds escaping as you open the door. The aviary floor is best covered with concrete slabs or at least gravel so that it can be hosed down. Bare earth is a breeding ground for bacteria. You cannot include shrubs and their like

A typical outdoor bird aviary. Aviaries like this one are suitable for cockatiels, canaries, pigeons and doves. ▶

A pair of lutinos (see page 25) on a perch of variable thicknesses. ◀

Yellow pearl cockatiels. ←

in a cockatiel aviary because these birds would soon destroy them, but a few natural branches should be included. Do not clutter an aviary but ensure there is a good open line of flight for the birds to go from one end to the other.

Site an aviary so it receives the benefit of the morning sunshine. Avoid placing it under trees because these will present many problems. They continually drop water into the flight long after it has stopped raining. Wild birds perched above the aviary will continually drop fecal matter into it with the attendant health hazards. The area will generally be damp, encouraging fungal growth. In the warm weather trees will attract flies.

If the site is open it should be given protection against harsh weather, either by a wall, fence or cladding on the flight. Ideally, the aviaries should be such that you can see them from the most used room in your home. There are many super extras you can purchase for an aviary, including ionizers (to keep the air fresh), light dimmers, fire alarms, coolers, and heaters. You can even have a remote camera set up so you can keep your eye on the

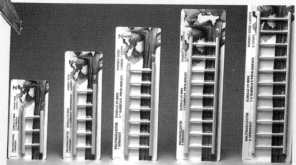

Wooden bird ladders are necessary for cockatiels. ◆

Gravel paper is highly recommended for the bottom of the cockatiel cage. ◆

birds when you are in your home. Try to visit a number of breeders who have good aviary setups before you invest in your own. It is also worthwhile subscribing to one of your national avicultural magazines as these are packed with useful information that can prove to be very helpful to you.

Breeding

Breeding cockatiels is both exciting and fulfilling. There is a great sense of achievement in seeing for the first time a number of fledglings leave the nest. There is also the anticipation of wondering how good this year's crop of youngsters will turn out if you are an exhibitor, or what colors you will get from given pairings. However, if you decide to breed your birds you should ensure you have the extra accommodation required for the offspring, and be prepared for the extra feeding costs.

There is little point in breeding for its own sake, so you should have an objective. Only breed with sound birds of good quality, otherwise you will only get second-rate babies which have little value. Never breed from overweight hens, out-of-condition stock, or that which is ill or only just recovering from an illness. Never pair two very young birds together—one of them should always have had previous breeding experience.

Young nestling cockatiels are born naked when their eggs hatch; it takes a week before their feathers become fully evident.

Do not be over ambitious in your initial efforts; more than one person has taken on more birds than they later would have wished. It is better to be able to cope well and be enthusiastic than find oneself buried in stock, overcrowding, high seed bills and a lot of problems! Be prepared for many disappointments because things rarely go as you might have wished them to. Birds are living creatures, not breeding machines.

A magnificent specimen of a pearl cockatiel. See page 27 for more information on pearls. ◆

Seed bells are made especially for cockatiels. ◆

Breeding Facts

The cockatiel is sexually mature before it is a year old. However, breeding from very young birds has little to recommend, so wait until the season following the year of their birth before pairing up stock. Once a breeding pair has been established the birds can remain together for the rest of their lives. Cockatiels develop very strong pair bonds which should ideally be left intact. Be sure the birds have been well exercised in an outdoor aviary for some months before they are expected to breed; they will then be in strong breeding condition. Too many hobbyists concentrate on birdroom breeding just to increase the number of chicks they can obtain. The results are seen in weedy birds that quickly succumb to problems when they are expected to winter outdoors in temperate climates. Go for a few birds but which are really of a strong vigorous constitution—it will pay in the long run as your birds will be in demand.

The cockatiel clutch is usually of five eggs but may be as few as two or three or as many as seven. Both parents share in sitting on the eggs and the incubation period is normally 19 days, but may end a day or two later if the weather is cool. The chicks fledge when they are 42-55 days old, depending on how good their parents are and what the weather is like. They will then be fed by the parents for maybe another 10-14 days, so are independent at about the age of eight to ten weeks. Their eyes open around the eighth day and feathers start appearing just after this time. If they are to be ringed the rings are fitted when they are about 10 days old. You can obtain the correct rings from specialist suppliers or your national club.

Of the eggs laid you can expect about 50-65% to result in chicks. Unless you are very

A nice bordered cinnamon pearl. See page 27 for more information. ◆

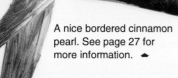

The young chicks are almost fully feathered. Their eggs took 19 days to hatch and take about 3 weeks to look like this. ◆

fortunate, be prepared for the reality that only rarely will all the chicks survive, especially with large clutches. The nest box required is a tall one, though cockatiels are extremely accommodating on this matter. The favored dimensions will be about 25cm square by 45cm high (10x10x18in), but somewhat smaller boxes will suffice. A small hole is placed towards the top of the box and a hinged lid to the box is useful for checking on the youngsters. The nest box is lined with some sawdust and may be fitted with a wooden concave.

You will appreciate that there is a great deal more to breeding cockatiels than can be mentioned in such a small book, but it is hoped that discussion will give you a brief insight into this aspect. You are strongly recommended to obtain a more detailed text if breeding appeals to you. Do remember the point stated about birds not being machines. If you obtain two to three clutches in a season be satisfied with this and let the birds have a needed rest in order to build up their strength for the following season. Excessive breeding will only result in progressively smaller clutches and more sickly offspring. Keep detailed records of your breeding results.

The parents feed the young, as shown here, for another 10-14 days. ☜

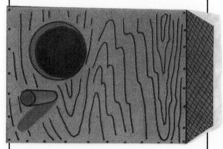

A cockatiel nest box may be purchased at your local pet shop. ☜

A three-week old pearl chick. ☞

A normal male mating with a pearl female. The mounting is very fast, perhaps lasting for 5 seconds. ☞

The top of the nest box is removed so the chicks can come out after six weeks or more.

Regardless of their colors, cockatiels are excellent pet birds if purchased young. Birds which are already finger tamed when you buy them are worth much more than untamed birds.

The Pet Cockatiel

It is advisable to have a cage for your pet before you collect the cockatiel.
The seller of the bird will supply you with a suitable carton to transport the bird home in. Collect the cockatiel as early in the day as possible so it has time to settle into its quarters before it gets dark. Once home open the cage door and place the transport box such that as you open it the youngster will fly in. You can now leave the bird to clamber around the cage and generally inspect it. It may simply flutter into a corner, but eventually it will start to move around.

Carry on with your normal routine and do instruct children not to pester the bird by constantly tapping the cage bars or standing too close to the cage. It is a traumatic time for the youngster so give it a while to settle down. The food and water containers should have been filled before the bird was placed into the cage.

Finger Taming

It may well be that your pet is already finger tame, but if not this is easy to achieve with a young cockatiel. Place your hand slowly into the cage and move it towards the bird. Be sure it can see your hand at all times. By placing your index finger under its chest, just above its legs, it will step onto this. It may reach down and place its beak on your finger because parrots use their beak rather like a hand, or third foot. They also test unknown objects with their beak.

If the bird is nervous, simply go through the process at a slower pace, maybe over one or two days, but generally a young cockatiel can be finger tamed in no time at all. Once it is quite happy to step onto your finger it can then be allowed out of its cage.

Potential Hazards

There are many hazards you must safeguard against in the average home.

1. See that open fires and chimneys are covered with a suitable mesh guard.

2. Ensure that fish tanks have a hood on them.

3. Leave no windows open, and ideally, until your pet is aware it cannot fly through glass, place some mesh curtain over the windows so it will not crash into the glass and injure or even kill itself. This is most likely during its first few flights as it will panic a little.

4. Keep the kitchen door closed—this room holds many dangers. If the kitchen is part of the living area be sure there are no boiling pans on the cooker, or ventilation fans operating, or gas rings lit, when your pet is flying at liberty.

5. Always be present when your bird is at liberty and if other pets, such as dogs or cats, are part of the family.

Handling

Always be very gentle when handling the cockatiel. Talk softly to it and do not let children run around thus frightening it. Being such a gentle bird, the cockatiel will soon sit on your hand, shoulder, or head quite happily. They like

◗ This same bird, however, makes an excellent pet which thrives on hand feeding. The cage is not proper because the wires are vertical and not horizontal.

◆ All mutant color varieties can be mated to each other to produce one-of-a-kind colored cockatiels like this one.

17

It is best to handle your pet cockatiel on your finger.

playing with many small toys and especially enjoy nibbling on twigs. Be sure toys are not of thin plastic that might be chewed into pieces and swallowed. Once you have a tame cockatiel you may decide to add another because parrots can become very much part of your home. However, avoid mixing large powerful parrots with the cockatiel.

Talking

Any person who purchases a parrot specifically in the hope of it talking is very foolish. Even known excellent talking species may never say a word. The beauty of a parrot is its nature. You can teach a parrot to talk by repeating simple words over and over again. If it then mimics these you can regard this as a

Once it has a grip on your finger, hold your hand steady so the bird will have confidence and be secure when on your hand.

When you have your bird on a perch, press your finger against its breast to force it to grasp your finger.

bonus. The cockatiel cannot be regarded as an especially noted talker, but may mimic a few words. Only try to teach it to talk for a few minutes at a time, and only when you are alone with it and there are no distractions—in the evening is a good time.

Wing Clipping

Not all parrot owners agree on the need to clip a bird's wings. You must decide for yourself on this matter based on the degree of risk in your home of the bird escaping. Do remember that if a cockatiel does escape, and has trimmed wings, it is unable to get away from potential dangers— such as dogs, cats, foxes or other animals. Conversely, with the full power of flight, if your pet escapes it is unlikely you will ever see it again as this species tends to panic and lose itself. The possible middle road is to have your vet, or an experienced breeder, trim the flights such that there is some lift but not enough for the bird to travel very far. I do not favor trimming one wing only as this totally discourages the bird from ever attempting to fly, which surely is a rather selfish attitude to take. Trimmed feathers will be replaced at each annual molt.

You will find that if you give your bird lots of attention, and freedom, all of your friends will soon be wanting one of these gorgeous parrots.

If your bird's wings are clipped, it must stay on your finger since it cannot fly. Thus wing clipping aids in taming. ▸

The flight feathers on this cockatiel's wing have been clipped off to half their length. Eventually the bird molts and new feathers come in...then it can fly again. ☛

This is the normal color of a wild cockatiel. It is fully feathered and perfectly healthy. Birds should *look* healthy. ▶

Preventing Illness

Your cockatiel can probably suffer from as many ailments and diseases as you or I can. The objective is, therefore, to try and prevent these. In the event that your pet does become ill, the only worthwhile course is to let your vet deal with matters. Do not try and make a diagnosis yourself, nor listen to "so-called" bird experts. If they are not veterinarians, they are neither trained nor equipped to deal with avian diseases, regardless of what they might tell you.

Sound Husbandry

Your main line of defense in preventing illness is always by practicing sound general husbandry. The single bird kept as a pet is far less likely to become ill than is an aviary bird. This is because it lives in a

Options such as cockatiel claw clippers (left) and cockatiel cold remedies are available at your local pet shop. ◆

much more controlled environment. It is not at risk to disease by direct transmission from other aviary or wild birds. Nor is it quite as exposed to potential pathogens (disease-causing organisms) and to such pests as fungi and various parasites. Husbandry covers all aspects of avian management from feeding and accommodation to hygiene and care in avoiding situations that will stress your pet. It also means inspecting your birds on a regular (daily) basis and then dealing promptly with any problems seen.

Hygiene

Cages and aviaries should be cleaned as often as possible and certainly once a week. Do not leave gathered debris and husked seeds lying

Cockatiels must have gravel in their crops in order to grind the seeds. Cockatiel gravel is essential to the health of your bird. ◀

around in bags—burn or otherwise dispose of this rubbish. Wash perches down as soon as they are seen to be dirty. As soon as they are unable to be cleaned properly, they should be replaced. Replace any cracked food or water containers. Clean feeding dishes daily. If you have aviaries, be sure the dishes are placed back in the same aviary they came from— number the aviary and its utensils.

Be aware you can easily transport bacteria from pet shops, the vet's office, bird shows and your

Your local pet shop has health aids for cockatiels.

friend's aviaries back to your home on your clothes. Always wash your hands before and after handling birds. Use disposable surgical gloves when handling ill birds. Store all food where it cannot be contaminated with the droppings of birds, mice, or rats.

Know Your Birds

Birds are like people in that every one of them has its own little mannerisms. Some are very active, some are more lazy. Some are aggressive, others are very timid. Some really hog on food, others nibble steadily. The only way you can know about these aspects is if you devote plenty of time to watching them. In this way, you will soon notice if any are not acting in a normal manner. This will be sufficient grounds to isolate them for further observation—or contact your vet if it is a single pet bird.

It is always better to play safe than to put matters off for another day. It may only take a day for a condition to worsen and prove fatal. Birds do

◄ A normal colored female in excellent health.

◄ Millet sprays are natural cockatiel foods.

not readily display clinical signs for many illnesses, so by the time they do, things are usually getting pretty bad.

Quarantine (Isolation)

If you decide to add other birds to your collection, work on the theory that you will assume they are ill until you are satisfied they are not. If more aviary owners adopted this view, the number of deaths in an aviary would fall. Try to place new arrivals well away from your stock for about 14 days, which will usually be long enough for most illnesses to show themselves. Likewise, if a bird is looking ill, remove it as quickly as possible from other birds. Heat is one of nature's great healers, so apply this via an infrared lamp placed in front of the cage, or simply by hanging a lighted bulb over the cage. Be sure water is always available. Aviary owners might consider investing in one of the better hospital cages now available, as long as it is large enough to accommodate a cockatiel.

Light pearl female. ◄

Cockatiels love swings. Many bird owners consider them a cage necessity. ◄

A pair of pearl pied cockatiels. ►

If your bird displays any of the following symptoms, you can assume it is unwell—the more so if the symptoms are together.

1. Sitting with feathers all ruffled up and both feet on the perch with the head drooped into its upper chest.

2. Showing a discharge from either its eyes or its nostrils.

3. Swollen cere (the fleshy area above the beak).

4. Very runny fecal matter or that which is stained with blood.

5. Difficulty in breathing.

6. Difficulty in remaining on its perch.

7. Constantly scratching itself—usually indicative of external parasites which can lead to secondary, and more dangerous, conditions.

8. Abnormal behavior, including lack of interest in its food.

9. Cuts or abrasions.

In any of the above instances contact your vet immediately. If an aviary bird dies without displaying signs of illness it is wise to have a postmortem conducted via your vet. This may save others of your stock if the cause can be identified.

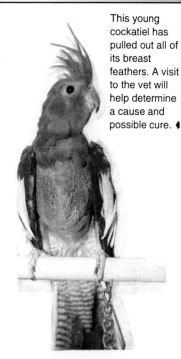

This young cockatiel has pulled out all of its breast feathers. A visit to the vet will help determine a cause and possible cure.

If your bird displays any abnormal symptoms, contact your vet as soon as possible.

This cockatiel has a bad eye. A visit to the veterinarian should not be delayed.

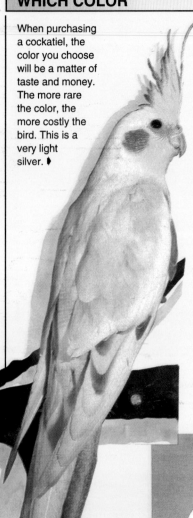

When purchasing a cockatiel, the color you choose will be a matter of taste and money. The more rare the color, the more costly the bird. This is a very light silver. ◗

Which Color?

There are over a dozen color varieties in the cockatiel but a number of these look rather similar. Beauty is obviously in the eye of the beholder, but most people are likely to agree that the lutino, the pied, the lutino pearl, and the albino are the most striking birds. Certainly good examples of these will be more costly than other colors. All mutations will be more expensive than normals (unless the latter are top quality exhibition birds).

What Are Mutations?

Color, and all other features of a bird, are passed from one generation to the next via genes. When captive animals are bred in large numbers, it increases the likelihood of the genes mutating, especially in terms of their color. Mutation is essential for evolution to take place. It results in the genes steadily changing in the way they express themselves. If the changes prove beneficial in the environment at that time, then they are retained—if not, they die out. It is a continuum which ultimately

Your pet shop has lots of books on cockatiels published by T.F.H.Publications, Inc., the publisher of this book. ◗

24

leads to speciation, the creation of new species.

In the wild, most color mutations do not prove beneficial to a species, so they are lost. In captivity, these can be retained and improved by selective breeding for modifiers—other genes that increase the intensity of the main mutation on a buildup basis. Color varieties are thus created both by major natural mutations and also by cross breeding with these. The more natural mutations there are, the more permutations that become possible.

Lutino

The effect of this mutation is to remove the black pigment. This leaves you with a gorgeous white bird with a yellow crest and orange cheek spots. There is actually some yellow diffusion in the white and this can be selected to produce an almost yellow bird. The color is sometimes, and incorrectly, termed an albino, which it cannot be as it obviously carries colored pigments. It is termed a sex-linked mutation because the gene responsible is carried on the sex chromosomes, and this fact must be considered when calculating theoretical expectations. A hen cannot be split (carrying in her genetic makeup) for a sex-linked color; she is either a lutino or a non-lutino. Lutino is partially epistatic in its action,

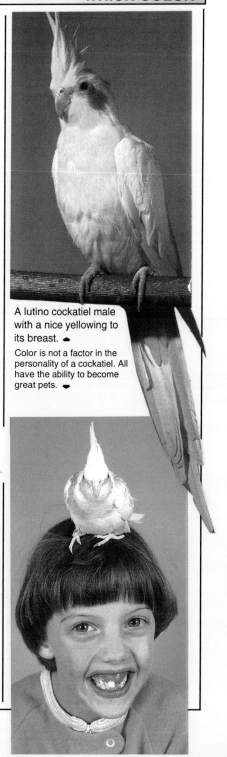

A lutino cockatiel male with a nice yellowing to its breast. ▲

Color is not a factor in the personality of a cockatiel. All have the ability to become great pets. ◆

A lutino cockatiel. ◀

A normal colored male. This is the color of the wild cockatiels in Australia. ←

A poor quality silver cockatiel. ←

which means that when paired with most other mutations it will mask their presence.

Pied

This mutation results in certain areas losing black pigmentation. The effect is most pleasing in a well-marked example. Ideally, the bird should have clear (white) tail and wing feathers, also a clear mask carrying no gray markings. The rest of the bird should show yellow where it replaces the gray. The gene is totally unpredictable in how much pied there will be on the bird. This might be restricted to a tiny area on the underside of the tail such that the bird looks normal. It corresponds to white spotting (piebald, skewbald) seen in other animals (cat, hamster, horse, etc.).

The color is recessive in transmission, meaning that a bird of either sex can carry the gene for pied in its genotype (genetic makeup) without this being visually apparent. Such a bird is described as being split, denoted with an oblique line. That before the line is visual, that behind is carried but not visual.

A closeup showing the feather development around the eye and face. ←

Pearl

This very variable mutation can also look super in a good example. The effect of the mutant gene is to remove just some of the gray near the tips of each feather to create a scalloped effect. The tail feathers are totally affected in most instances. The ideal is to have yellow markings, but often they are a mixture. Heavily marked examples are called lacewings. Poorly marked examples tend to look rather blotched and unattractive. Pearled males will lose much of the pearling with successive molts; this is due to the heavier density of melanin in males. It is a sex-influenced color.

Cinnamon

The effect of this sex-linked mutation is to reduce the gray-black pigment to brown. This can result in a pleasing appearance in a well-marked bird. When coupled with other mutations, such as in the cinnamon pied, it can produce birds of a very delicate shade.

Dilute

In this bird the gene responsible dilutes the strength of the melanin so it becomes paler. If both of a bird's genes at this locus are for dilute, this will make the bird even lighter in shade—it is termed a double factor bird for its color. When the gene is present, the normal gray becomes paler (termed silver), as does the cinnamon. The mutation is dominant in its mode of transmission—which means that its effect will become apparent even though it is present in single gene form (it is thus never carried in split form-–

Both of the birds shown here are possessors of the dilute gene which made their colors lighter than normal. This dilution only affects the black coloration (melanin), thus the yellow and orange are in full strength in both birds. ◀

A beautiful pearl. ➥

Your birds' cage should be sprayed regularly with mite and lice spray to be sure they stay free of harmful parasites. ▶

This is a dilute pearl. ▶

if a bird has the gene it will affect the color of that bird). There is now also a second mutation that produces silver and this is termed recessive silver.

Whiteface

This mutation results in the removal of pigment from the facial area. It usually produces a bird that has an entirely white face. Some may still show a graying effect, but this will clear with selective breeding—there are of course no cheek spots. In itself, it cannot be regarded as an especially striking mutation. When combined with the lutino mutation it is possible to produce an

albino--there is no true natural albino in the cockatiel at this time. As in some other species, one must produce it by selective permutations. Some of these albinos will not be pure white as might be expected (though they are red-eyed). As with most albinos, there are usually some traces of yellowing. This can be removed by a careful breeding program.

Recombinations

By recombining any of the mutations you can produce some super birds (as well as some that fail to impress). The lutino pearl is beautiful if well marked—a combination of white with yellow pearling, all set off by the orange cheek spots. The pearl pied is another combination that is effective if good. This equally applies to the cinnamon pied. In the coming years other mutations will occur, not so much with color but with its placement. This will create other patterns, such as half siders and banded cockatiels. The cockatiel offers tremendous possibilities for breeding—on top of which you have its delightful character.

A Lutino Cockatiel. Although this variety is predominantly white, it is not a true albino; to be a true albino it would need to have pink eyes and no coloration. ◂

A beautiful normal cockatiel. ◂

Partially dilute normally colored cockatiel. The gray is lighter than normal.

A gray and gray pearl with yellow make attractive cockatiel mutations. ◆

Exhibition

The show side of birds is both interesting and exciting. Even if you never show your cockatiels you might still become addicted to visiting shows. You can keep your eye on the standard of the stock, maybe purchase young birds, or maintain friendships with those you get to know. As an exhibitor/breeder you will find it is a means of meeting potential buyers of your surplus birds, apart from the thrill of picking up wins or places if your stock is good enough.

Types of Show

A bird show can range from a small informal club show restricted to members to a major exhibition which may be spread over two days. The show may cater to all types of birds, or it may be limited to parrotlike birds, or even just to cockatiels. Shows limited to cockatiels are organized by the cockatiel society of your country, of which there may be more than one.

Show Classes

The larger the show the more classes will be scheduled for cockatiels. There may be classes for each mutational form, plus the normals, as well as for each sex. A small show might simply have two divisions—one for normals and one for mutational colors. Class winners go forward to compete for the best bird in the show. In the UK, the judges go around to the cages in order to judge. This is done behind closed doors—the public and the exhibitors not being allowed in until after judging is over. In the USA, the judging is not done behind closed doors, however; all are invited to watch.

Show Cage and Training

All cockatiels are exhibited in special show cages which are painted black with white or pastel blue on the inside. Show birds must be trained from an early age. They must be steady in the cage and not be frightened by the many people who will be looking at them at close quarters. This requires much time devoted to practice, with the exhibitor inviting friends to view his or her birds in order to duplicate show conditions. Cage training is a slow but gradual process.

The birds must obviously be in superb condition, which requires months of preparation. The plumage must

This perch is ideal since it has variable thick-nesses. ▸

Gravel paper is necessary for the bottom of your cockatiel cage. Yes, they even make gravel paper for round cage bottoms, too. ▾

If your birds stay crouched and puffed up they are under stress (unless they are sleeping) and they should NOT be taken for exhibition. ◂

GRAVEL PAPER

For all Hagen Hundred cages

You don't need fancy color varieties to win a show. A normal colored bird in good plumage has an excellent chance in the local bird shows.

Cockatiels are now shown at budgerigar exhibitions. This cockatiel won a lot of awards at a budgie competition in which cockatiels were shown in their own class.

be immaculate and spraying it with tepid water is very useful in the weeks prior to exhibitions. If team classes are entered, this means one of each sex, they should be as near an identical pair as possible. This requires matching up birds very carefully, so it is not always a case of pairing your best bird up with another.

How to Become an Exhibitor

The best way to proceed is to firstly visit a few bird shows to see what you think of it all. If it appeals to you, then join your cockatiel or parrot society. Attend meetings and you will be advised how to prepare and enter any show. You will also receive advice on how to prepare the bird and many other aspects of keeping cockatiels. Even if you do not exhibit, membership in national and local clubs is highly recommended.

Pied cockatiels that are to be exhibited should be symmetrical in their markings.